SandCastle™ Synonyms

The Pickle Is Dilly, Cool and Chilly!

Tracy Kompelien

Consulting Editor, Diane Craig, M.A./Reading Specialist

ABDO Publishing Company

Published by ABDO Publishing Company, 4940 Viking Drive, Edina, Minnesota 55435.

Printed in the United States.

Credits
Edited by: Pam Price
Curriculum Coordinator: Nancy Tuminelly
Cover and Interior Design and Production: Mighty Media
Photo Credits: Shutterstock, Steve Wewerka

Library of Congress Cataloging-in-Publication Data
Kompelien, Tracy, 1975-
The pickle is dilly, cool and chilly! / Tracy Kompelien.
p. cm. -- (Synonyms)
ISBN-13: 978-1-59928-730-0
ISBN-10: 1-59928-730-7
1. English language--Synonyms and antonyms--Juvenile literature. I. Title.

PE1591.K65 2007
428.1--dc22

2006031422

SandCastle™ books are created by a professional team of educators, reading specialists, and content developers around five essential components–phonemic awareness, phonics, vocabulary, text comprehension, and fluency–to assist young readers as they develop reading skills and strategies and increase their general knowledge. All books are written, reviewed, and leveled for guided reading, early reading intervention, and Accelerated Reader® programs for use in shared, guided, and independent reading and writing activities to support a balanced approach to literacy instruction.

Let Us Know

SandCastle would like to hear your stories about reading this book. What is your favorite page? Was there something hard that you needed help with? Share the ups and downs of learning to read. We want to hear from you! To get posted on the ABDO Publishing Company Web site, send us e-mail at:

sandcastle@abdopublishing.com

SandCastle Level: Fluent

A synonym is a word that has the same or a similar meaning as another word.

Here is a good way to remember what a synonym is:

synonym
=
same
=
similar

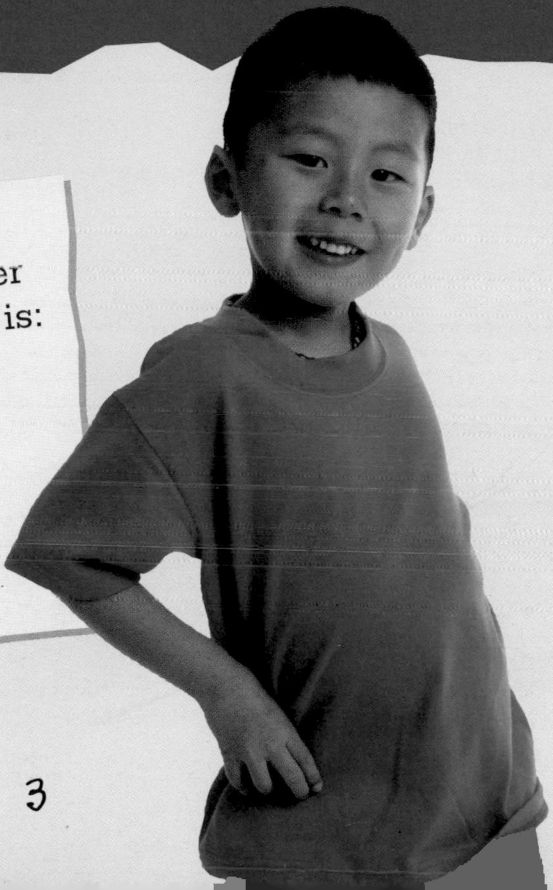

synonyms

The lettuce is crisp.

firm

crunchy

fresh

brittle

synonyms

Sara's malt is creamy.

smooth

silky

velvety

rich

synonyms

The soup is hot.

warm
scorching
boiling
burning
steamy
fiery

synonyms

The pizza is tasty.

delicious

yummy

delectable

delightful

scrumptious

synonyms

The peppers are spicy.

peppery

hot

zesty

flavorful

synonyms

The pasta is warm. The noodles are steamy. The cheese is creamy and delicious. Steve likes his pasta really cheesy!

Can you find any synonyms for the word warm in the paragraph above?

synonyms

The ice-cream sundae is rich. Nan puts on creamy chocolate. She likes three scoops of velvety ice cream in a cold dish. This is a special sundae!

Can you find any synonyms for the word rich in the paragraph above?

synonyms

The salsa is zesty. Peppers make the salsa hot. Heather thinks the salsa is too spicy to eat. She eats plain chips instead.

Can you find any synonyms for the word zesty in the paragraph above?

What synonyms can you use to describe the delicious brownies?

Glossary

brittle – easily broken, cracked, or snapped.

delicious – very pleasing to taste or smell.

fiery – being hot or red like a fire.

scrumptious – delightful and delicious.

velvety – being soft and smooth like velvet.

zesty – having a lively, spicy flavor.

Words I Know

Nouns

A noun is a person, place, or thing.

Verbs

A verb is an action or being word.

Words I Know

Adjectives

An adjective describes something.

boiling, 9
brittle, 5
burning, 9
cheesy, 15
cold, 17
creamy, 7, 15, 17
crisp, 5
crunchy, 5
delectable, 11
delicious, 11, 15, 20
delightful, 11
fiery, 9
firm, 5
flavorful, 13
fresh, 5
his, 15
hot, 9, 13, 19
peppery, 13
plain, 19
rich, 7, 17
scorching, 9
scrumpious, 11
silky, 7
smooth, 7
special, 17
spicy, 13, 19
steamy, 9, 15
tasty, 11
this, 17
three, 17
warm, 9, 15
what, 20
velvety, 7, 17
yummy, 11
zesty, 13, 19

Proper Nouns

A proper noun is the name of a person, place, or thing.

Heather, 19
Nan, 17
Sara, 7
Steve, 15

About SandCastle™

A professional team of educators, reading specialists, and content developers created the SandCastle™ series to support young readers as they develop reading skills and strategies and increase their general knowledge. The SandCastle™ series has four levels that correspond to early literacy development in young children. The levels are provided to help teachers and parents select the appropriate books for young readers.

Emerging Readers
(no flags)

Beginning Readers
(1 flag)

Transitional Readers
(2 flags)

Fluent Readers
(3 flags)

These levels are meant only as a guide. All levels are subject to change.

ABDO
Publishing Company

To see a complete list of SandCastle™ books and other nonfiction titles from ABDO Publishing Company, visit www.abdopublishing.com or contact us at:
4940 Viking Drive, Edina, Minnesota 55435 • 1-800-800-1312 • fax: 1-952-831-1632